ray troll's

shocking

fish tales

fish, romance, and death

in pictures by ray troll

and words by brad matsen

alaska northwest books™

anchorage • seattle

Library of Congress Cataloging-in-Publication Data
Troll, Ray, 1954–
      [Shocking fish tales]
      Ray Troll's shocking fish tales : fish, romance, and death in
pictures / by Ray Troll ; text by Brad Matsen.
          p.   cm.
      ISBN 0-88240-416-4
      1. Troll, Ray, 1954–   —Themes, motives.   2. Fishes in art.
3. Fishes.   4. Fishing.   I. Matsen, Bradford.   II. Title.
N6537.T69A4   1991
760'.092—dc20   91-16788
                                                   CIP

Note: For all reproduced artworks, dimensions are given in inches, and height precedes width.

Edited by Marlene Blessing
Cover and book design by Kate L. Thompson
Lettering by Carl Smool
Photographs of Ray Troll artwork by Ray Troll, Normand Dupre, and Joe Manfredini

Covers: *Fish Worship* (front cover); *Humpies from Hell* (back cover).

Alaska Northwest Books™
A division of GTE Discovery Publications, Inc.
22026 20th Avenue S.E.
Bothell, WA 98021

Printed and bound in Korea
through Overseas Printing Corporation,
San Francisco, California

For my parents, Mary and Ray   R. T.

For Colleen, who took me salmon fishing   B. C. M.

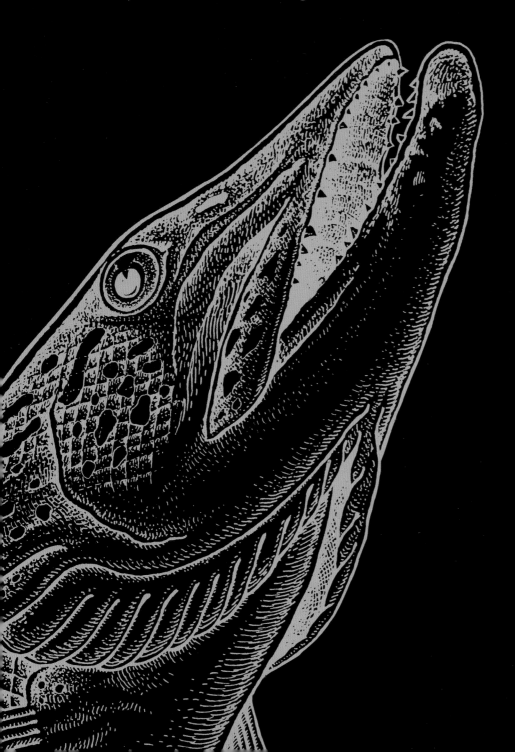

RAPTURE OF THE DEEP

RAPTURE OF
THE DEEP, 1985.
Mixed media, 36 x 48.

Stream of Contents

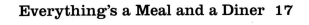
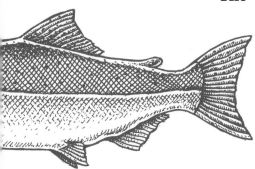

HOWLING DOGS

HOWLING DOGS, 1989.
Pen and ink, 9 x 9.

A Day at the Beach with Ray and Brad

Ray and I had been gazing into the tank of Pacific spiny lumpsuckers for about five minutes when it hit me that I ought to tell you about our trip to the People's Aquarium in Port Townsend, Washington, to introduce us and give you some idea how we feel about fish. Pacific spiny lumpsuckers are roundish, odd little numbers about an inch and a half long that flutter like hummingbirds to move around and, when at rest, attach themselves to the glass or something else with an adhesive disk on their bellies. Ray Troll is about five ten, sliding into middle age, with a beard and distinctive high-tide hairline, and I look enough like him on a bad morning to take the rap for him in a police lineup. One time we walked into a tavern and a guy, apparently firmly aground after an afternoon at the bar, slurred, "Brothers. Right?" as we walked in.

PLANET OCEAN AND THE ANTIFREEZE POLLOCK

Watching the lumpsuckers, which are abundant in the Pacific from Washington to Alaska and along the Aleutians to the Siberian coast, Ray is well into a rambling fantasy about Lumpsucker City in the tank, which also includes another of his favorites, grunt sculpins. The curator of the place, really called the Port Townsend Marine Science Center, is saying to Ray, "I have your postcards all over my bedroom," and an assistant is standing there, too, pointing out another critter in the tank. "There's the one that really grabs me," he says. "An alabaster nudibranch," and we stare at a couple of inches of spectacularly translucent invertebrate, a mollusk without a shell, waving its tendrils to some secret rhythm.

The scene was typical of what you get when a few fish addicts gather around a tank, fascination on the loose, all of us trying to out-species each other, sharing the delights of Planet Ocean. This little

9

aquarium on a somewhat dilapidated dock where Puget Sound hangs a big left to become the Strait of Juan de Fuca, and then the Pacific Ocean, was started spontaneously by a group of volunteers in the early eighties. It operates on just the vapors of money for the most part, but the curators, docents, and teachers who run classes for kids vibrate when they talk about thirty thousand people passing through the place in 1990.

For no charge, unless you want to make a donation, you can wander around a single, chilly room with a latticework of homemade plumbing that gurgles overhead and stroke sea stars that have lived in the flat, waist-high touch tanks for as long as the center has existed. You can risk alien sensations and touch the utterly unlikely sea cucumbers, or watch a box crab make a living behind a pile of rock as it waits for something yummy to drift by in the current. You can marvel at squid locomotion in homemade tanks or the random dances of hundreds of young walleye pollock that, somehow, survived a freeze that killed almost every other fish in the place in the winter of 1990.

Frank D'Amor, the curator, will tell you he mourns the loss of a pet rockfish he'd grown from a two-incher to an eight-incher, a species that can live a hundred years or more. "It would eat out of my hand," Frank says, remembering the freeze and the rockfish. He says the antifreeze pollock slowed down a bit when the tank iced over, but were voracious and ready to boogie when the weather warmed up. "We just chipped the ice off the surface and look at them now."

In the tank, the three-inch juvenile pollock flash and hover like silver lights on a screen, while two thousand miles north on the Bering Sea, the largest fishing fleet in the world is trawling for a half-billion or so of their older relatives. Pollock are the keystone of a human food industry second to none, and we barely even know where the fish breed and mature or how many of them there are. The lab volunteers collected their tankful from the eelgrass in the nearby shallows, where major-league experts in the federal fisheries bureaucracy told them they'd never find any.

John Dobson, the great astronomer, is fond of saying, "You can't begin to understand the universe unless you look at it once in a while," and he backs up his philosophy by building affordable telescopes for the masses. Frank, Jack McAnally, and the others who tend the little seaside aquarium transmit their fascination to thousands of fellow earthlings, and surely looking at the sea and its creatures helps us grasp an understanding of life as we know it.

At the marine center, an ambitious project is in the works, finally pulling Ray and me from the pollock to the wall where a local artist named Diane Bordman — also a volunteer — is painting a mural that depicts no less than the timeline of life on earth. The undulating ribbon begins at the front door, turns a corner, and runs along one entire side of the room, a projection of evolution on the scale of a single year, and it's about two-thirds done. Nothing even close to life on land has occurred to this point, billions of years into life in the sea, but we've emerged from single-cell to multicell organisms, part plant, part animal, mostly algae. Frank takes us into the back room, where the last section is propped on a table. On the year scale, life didn't even leave the sea until December; the dinosaurs appear on December 21 and disappear December 26. Humans and the mammal gang don't show up until the last split seconds of December 31. "Fine-looking trilobites," Ray says of the complex life-form that preceded vertebrates.

After a couple of hours, Ray and I head for the car, ambling into the winter wind with Frank, who tells us about the Migrating Salmonmobile. In the summer, a 28-foot fiber glass fish, another volunteer project, is parked on the dock outside, touring schools when it's not at the marine center. You can walk up a ramp into its mouth and enter a replica of the riparian zone, streamside habitat complete with soundtrack to drive home the point, mainly to children, that salmon need streams to survive.

Frank tells us the salmonmobile is sponsored by sport and commercial fishing groups trying to encourage habitat protection, and we take off on a new streak of conversational fish frenzy, talking about fishing, a minor and typical variation on our theme. Both Ray and I are pretty hard-core fishermen, sometimes for sport, sometimes for money. Frank launches into a nostalgic reminiscence about his early days in Port Townsend, just ten years before, when he caught big salmon from the beach. He describes the lures he used, his voice trailing off as he tells us a salmon from the beach is real rare any more. We ask him what happened, and he says, simply, "People."

THE VERTEBRATE TRIBE

Fish are our ancestors. In 1938, a living coelacanth was caught off the mouth of the Chalumna River in South Africa, a five-foot, 127-pound, electric blue message from the sea. Until then, paleontologists had found lots of fossils of this curious fish with fins like legs, some as old as seventy million years, from all over the world, but never a living specimen. The coelacanth, thought to be extinct, was promptly dubbed "The Living Fossil"

and, with media fanfare reserved for the most profound discoveries, sent scientists and the general public into wild speculations.

It's the missing link, some said, evidence that one day a long time ago a coelacanth took it into its pea brain to come ashore and walk. Professor J. L. B. Smith, the ichthyologist who named the specimen *Latimeria chalumnae,* played down the missing link theory but nicknamed the creature "Old Fourlegs" because its bony fins looked a lot like legs. Eventually, more coelacanths were taken live, and after awhile, locals on the African coast began saying, "Oh, those. We've been eating them for years." Now, there's a group called the Society for the Preservation of Old Fish (S.P.O.O.F), a real scientific clearinghouse, which has reported on such relics as coelacanth jewelry in Portugal in the nineteenth century.

Over 90 percent of all animals with backbones are still fish, though. They have evolved and thrived to become the most successful class of creatures, which should surprise no one who realizes that seven-eighths of the earth's surface is covered by water. Naturally the life-form most synchronized with the rhythms of our misnamed home planet has adapted

The early human inhabitants of Southeast Alaska were inexorably bonded to salmon for survival and called their aquatic partners simply "swimmers." They called themselves, of course, Salmon People.

DANCE OF THE FISH CHARMERS, 1985. Colored pencil, 18 x 22.

to the aquatic environment. Coming ashore might have been a terrible mistake. Since most living things are more water than not, it is an advantage for an organism to live in a place like the sea in which it doesn't have to expend so much energy to conserve and produce water. Obviously, swimming or drifting around as part of a nourishing soup like the ocean beats scrabbling for nuts and berries in a forest and maintaining the heat-and-water machinery of landlubber bodies.

We mammals seem to be in business primarily to make, shed, and move water. More than one wit observing the inanities of the human condition has suggested that the thing we do best is move water around, and that, therefore, must be the main clue to the meaning of life. It's not hard to feel a bit shortchanged, though, if shuttling a few gallons from Bridgeport, Connecticut, to Seattle amounts to cosmic purpose — but then who knows? And the downside of being a fish is that you are both predator and prey, sometimes at different points in your life cycle, but often at the same time. This condition is largely responsible for the success and spectacular variety of the fishes because, as Darwin so shockingly pointed out 150 years ago, death is not only as natural as life, but essential to its development.

A fish like the coelacanth that is relatively unchanged over millions of years is rare, not only because there aren't many left, but because almost everything else in the sea changes constantly to adapt to shifting conditions. Geneticists like to use salmon cells for mutation studies because you can get them to do things in a few generations that would take eons to show up in mammals. The most amazing thing about fish, evolution, and the sea is that back there, way back there, our grandparents were plants.

A lot of flatfish like halibut are born with eyes on both sides of their bodies, one of which migrates to join its partner on the upside. They are masters of camouflage, with bodies usually snow white on the bottom and mottled on the top to imitate the sea floor.

THE AVENGING
HALIBUT, 1988.
Oil pastel and crayon,
40 x 32.

LURE OF THE DEEP,
1985.
Colored pencil, 22 x 30.

Everything's a Meal and a Diner

If you're a fish, "What is the meaning of life?" has two answers: eating and reproduction, in that order. Everything else a fish does rates a distant third, implications of the spirit notwithstanding. Things are complicated and a little bit risky for fish because whether you get to be a big tuna depends a lot on whether or not you got eaten as a little tuna.

Most fish are carnivorous and so have evolved physiology that allows them to variously consume flesh, bones, and plant matter, depending on who's eating who. But "All flesh is grass," as the saying goes, meaning that protein from cow or codfish starts with a plant at the bottom of the line. The closer you get to the base of the pyramid-shaped food web, the less likely you are to run into a lifetime carnivore.

WHO EATS WHO IN THE SEA

At some point, something has to eat the plankton or its only slightly more evolved descendants, krill and the smaller shrimps. The marine food web — a.k.a. the food chain, a much less elaborate linear concept of how stuff goes together — is delicately balanced, and interference at the wrong stage can really foul things up. The idea, for instance, that we can start tinkering with krill and the other animals in the lower tiers upon which everything else depends is horrifying. The next time you hear somebody talking about krill or brine shrimp as food for the supermarket, call the cops.

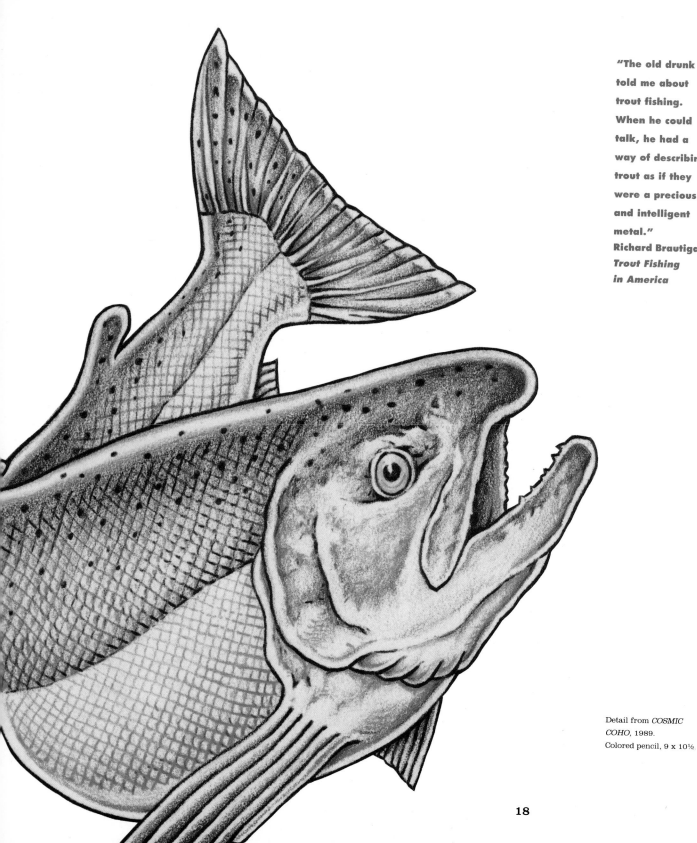

"The old drunk
told me about
trout fishing.
When he could
talk, he had a
way of describing
trout as if they
were a precious
and intelligent
metal."
Richard Brautigan,
*Trout Fishing
in America*

Detail from *COSMIC
COHO*, 1989.
Colored pencil, 9 x 10½.

18

THE NARRATIVE HOOK

Fish Lit 101 is a three-part course: books about fishing, books on how to fish, and books about fish themselves. Some books deal with more than one of those categories, and all are fashioned by writers who can be classified as members of a cult. No doubt editors seduced by the elegance of fly-fishing or the heady experiences of the deep sea also account for the forests of paper and rivers of ink expended on fish.

Most fish books have been written by men, probably because the duty of hunting, whether real or ritual, has fallen to the male of our species. There are notable exceptions, of course, including what is widely regarded as the very first piece of fish lit, *A Treatise on Fishing,* by Dame Juliana Berners, written in 1496. Regardless of the gender of the writer, fish books are about wilderness experience, companionship, respite from the pressures of life as we know it, and, not incidentally, the sheer thrill of hooking and landing a fish. And because the act of fishing merges the primitive with the practical, fish books usually yield a good dose of what can only be called philosophy.

FISH LIT 101

The first best seller about fishing was Izaak Walton's *The Compleat Angler or The Contemplative Man's Recreation, Being a Discourse on Rivers, Fishponds, Fish and Fishing not Unworthy of the Perusal of Most Anglers.* It started a tradition of long-windedness in the genre right off the bat, but has been in print pretty steadily since publication in 1654, and old Izaak, an Englishman, is known to most as the Father of Fish Lit.

Many books in the how-to-fish category read like they were written in an ancient foreign language, especially to beginners, who need them the most. In the mid-seventies, however, a guy named Sheridan Anderson wrote and illustrated a comic book on how to fly-fish — *The Curtis Creek*

Manifesto — and lightened things up a lot. Sheridan, a self-described artist, angler, wanderer, eternal foe of the work ethic, made his last cast in 1984 at much too young an age, but before departing cooked off his fish lit spectacular. It begins: "The major difficulty with most how-to fishing books is that of trying to figure out what the author is talking about."

The wisdom that follows on fifty elaborately illustrated pages can teach anybody to fish and like it. And eventually, Anderson reveals his attachment to mainstream fish lit by paying homage to bonding and mentors with classic ichthyosentiment: "If possible, latch onto a knowledgeable angler to go fishing with — a good teacher is worth more than all the angling literature ever written . . . Don't forget to send him a card on his birthday and a bottle of fancy booze at Christmas time."

Another deep pocket in the backwater of fish lit is, increasingly, good Fish Science Lit. When the real naturalists creep into fish lit, it is almost always with the revelation of some purer emotion toward the fish and their watery world, not so much fish as prey for human anglers. Catch Joy O. I. Spoczynska's marvelous *An Age of Fishes, Between Pacific Tides,* by Ed Ricketts and Joel Hedgepeth, or *The Erotic Ocean,* by Jack Rudloe.

A lot of people in the big-league fish lit record book are really just great writers who happened to love to fish and got sucked in by the bottomless supply of resonant metaphors in the woods and on boats. Ernest Hemingway was a totally addicted fisherman, and his *Old Man and the Sea* eventually won him the Nobel Prize because he crystallized the meaning of life as grace under pressure in a story about an old fisherman and a giant marlin. Zane Grey, whose real name was Pearl Gray (why did he change it?), wrote westerns more than fish lit, but he lived to fish and got famous for it. The truth is, any of the really big fish writers would have put rock polishing on the map if they'd have been into it. But one thing that fishing can do is keep you writing for the money to go fishing, which is a wicked circle of pain and self-indulgence.

PLENTY OF FISH
IN THE SEA, 1981.
Colored pencil, 15 x 20.

Fish Mind, Fish Art

The impulse to draw pictures of fish is as much a part of human existence as the only slightly more primitive urge to catch and eat them. For the earliest people, pictures of fish were, quite simply, pictures of food and spiritual entreaties that the seas, lakes, and rivers remain abundant. By comparing the fossil sludge and cave paintings of the ancients, it appears the art scene was not only a collection of images to court the gods of the hunt, but a product of curiosity about animals that move in the mysterious, airless environment we call water.

Since we began keeping records of pictures and why they got made, the significance of fish has surfaced in mythology, medicine, politics, art, and the rise and fall of empires. The Greek word for fish, ICThUS, is an acronym for the biblical phrase, "Jesus Christ, Son of God, Savior," and was a kind of secret password among the terrorized Christians of the Roman Empire. In the barbaric era of the crumbling Caesars when Christians were lion food if detected, the way you revealed yourself to a fellow cult member was to draw half the fish sign in the dirt with your foot as you talked. If the other guy completed the drawing with a swipe of his own, you could safely acknowledge your true beliefs. It's hard to imagine that the Romans didn't pick up on this, but that's the story, and now Christians put chrome fish on their automobiles.

And from an earlier era, the mummified bodies of Nile perch have

ROUSSEAU'S
HUMPIES, 1984.
Colored pencil, 7 x 9.

Some natives of the Pacific Northwest put ashes in the eyes of the season's first salmon so the spirit of the fish could not see them and tell the other fish to flee. A lot of modern commercial fishermen do just the opposite, returning the year's first fish to the sea so it can tell the others where to go.

MIDNIGHT RITUAL,
1985.
Mixed media, 36 x 48.

been found buried in the tombs of the Egyptian Pharaohs, and paintings and reliefs of fishers spearing their catch from the river are common on tomb walls. To the Egyptians, these symbolic sacrifices and earthly representations contributed to the magic re-creation of the earthly lives of the folks in the tomb when they made it to the hereafter. Apparently, the idea of a heaven including the abundance and fertility of fish was comforting.

Our fascination with the creatures in the sea intensified rather than diminished with the era of scientific exploration and discovery, and the desire to classify and catalog fish yielded the genre of scientific illustration. The early classifiers of sea life predate the Roman Empire, and though examples of grossly representative fish illustrations survive from early scientific history, not much remains from that period to show the elegance of detail in these creatures.

By the eighteenth century, however, at the dawning of the Age of Enlightenment in western Europe, human consciousness had embraced detail as critical to the scientific method. With religious fervor, scientists and illustrators took to the field. Drawings and paintings of fish from that period have assumed truly artistic proportions as new knowledge and the patina of age combine to elevate these early documentary works. Unscrupulous collectors are given to clipping the magnificent plates from otherwise undistinguished books, then selling the plates for big money.

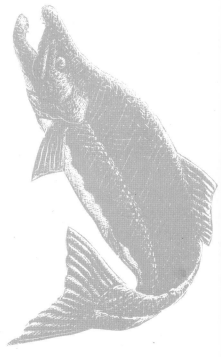

Interest in all things biological was intense during that time, and though abstract or fanciful representations of fish were not often created intentionally, some artists fudged a bit. The big commissions paid by wealthy collectors for illustrations of the rarest plant and animal curiosities sometimes led to imaginative renderings of exotic species, even some that never existed. One such enterprising naturalist included in his portfolio a "walking fish" he claimed to have caught on the sand and kept alive for three days in his house. He said the fish followed him everywhere "with great familiarity, like a dog." Even the legendary John J. Audubon once described and drew a dozen fish that existed only in his own mind as a joke played on a colleague.

In a sense, the accuracy of a representation of a fish is relative since these creatures are anything but stable in their appearance. Scientific drawings always come up short — no sooner are fish taken from the water or are spooked to move than they reveal a new light pattern on their bodies, or actually change their own colors. The variations in a single fish are truly endless.

Meanwhile, the artists and artisans of Native American and Asian societies worked on without the western European compulsion to describe and classify all of nature. For the Northwest Coast Indians, totemic carvings and later drawings took forms that can best be described as directly metaphoric. A stylized salmon in an arched pose with eggs shown in the belly, for instance, is not only a salmon but a symbol of fertility and prosperity, and the totem itself can eventually assume the full proportions of what it seeks to represent and become an actual being.

The original inhabitants of the Northwest Coast and the rest of the Pacific Rim correctly understood that fish are the direct predecessors of humans, though they didn't understand how eons of evolution fitted into the picture. Unencumbered by the tedious mechanics of natural evolution, a fish turning into a human could be understood as an instantaneous act of magic. To the Kwakiutl people of Vancouver Island, it was Halibut who threw off his skin, his tail, and his fins to emerge as the first man. To the Haida, man crawled out of a clamshell on Rose Spit at the northern end of Haida Gwaii, now called the Queen Charlotte Islands.

The images of fish that emerged from nineteenth- and twentieth-century Tlingit and Haida minds at about the same time as the Europeans were cataloging like crazy have survived, despite their lack of a written language to keep records and the vulnerability of the wood and fiber from which these images were made. Most of their fish impressions embellished utilitarian objects — hats, posts to hold up houses, ingeniously made chests for storage, ceremonial tools like rattles and headdresses, blankets, elaborate fishhooks, and totem poles to signal social position and to depict nothing less than the story of life on earth.

Totem poles, unique to the Northwest Coast, convey myths through forms that come from a rich spiritual universe with its own rules and conventions, rendered in the solid reality of the abundant giant spruce and cedars of the Pacific rain forest. Fish — particularly salmon — are dominant characters in the stories, along with Frog, Killer Whale, Eagle, and especially Raven, a free-lance spirit who can assume many forms at will.

One famous totem pole tells the story of the creation of salmon by a character called Fog Woman, who happens to be Raven's wife. The Kadjuk Pole, also called Chief Johnson's Pole, was set up in 1901 at its present location at the intersection of two main streets in Ketchikan, Alaska, a modern town that owes its existence, not surprisingly, to salmon and timber. The tale depicted on the Kadjuk Pole is an elaborate combination of treachery, magic, a bad spat between Raven and Fog Woman, and ultimately, the annual hordes of spawning salmon that meant the locals didn't have to eat bullheads or the less tasty fish of the shallows.

The sea creatures in the mythic art of the early coast dwellers show a reverence for the role of fish in basic survival. But after musing on the impulse to carve a salmon in a tree or explain its existence, you end up with one hard fact: fish is food. Now, in the late twentieth century, the five billion people on earth are gobbling seafood like never before, and fish pictures and totems proliferate. In art museums, galleries, sushi bars, shop windows, magazines, tattoos, and on T-shirts, key chains, and the tailgates of pickup trucks, images of fish represent our fascination with a parallel, watery world. Today's artists, like their predecessors, go beyond simple illustration into fantasy, folklore, and the spiritual associations of the aboriginal cultures whose survival depended on the oceans. Fish art lives.

The six kinds of Pacific Salmon are all *oncorhynchus* — hooknose is what it means — but all their local names make a great chant: *tshawytscha*, king, chinook, blackmouth, spring, and jack; *kisutch*, silver, coho, and northern; *keta*, chum, dog, and gator; *nerka*, sockeye, red, and blueback; *gorbuscha*, pink, humpback, and humpy; and, the rare one, *masu* or cherry. There's going to be a quiz at the end of the book.

DAUGHTER OF FOG,
1988.
Colored pencil, 30 x 19.

FISH SPIRIT JUJU,
1980.
Mixed media, 9 x 12.

The Church of How's-the-Fishing

FOOD, SPORT, AND STRANGE BEHAVIOR

TIME'S FUN WHEN YOU'RE HAVING FLIES, 1989. Pen, ink, and acrylic, 10 x 10.

If we caught something every time we wet a line, we'd call it catching instead of fishing. But not many fishermen will tell you they'll sell their tackle boxes and boats if they don't catch fish. Most of the seduction of fishing can be attributed to our hunting ancestry, the 99 percent of our history we spent as apex predators. Swordfish, marlins, lions, and eagles are also in the top layer of their own food clubs, but only humans join in battle with other apex predators for sport and practice on the lesser adversaries.

Since few modern humans who fish for sport will starve if they don't catch a meal, you have to look into myth, symbol, and ritual to understand why we take time from more essential activity to lust after salmon, bass, trout, or marlin. Respect for the prey accompanies the hunt and is probably critical to its success, though in modern sport the extremes of commerce are hardly respectful. Consider the cultural implications of a boatload of tourists in the Bahamas gooned out on rum at ten in the morning, unable even to hold a fishing rod when a marlin strikes.

A salmon fisherman in Southeast Alaska dragging out his tackle to clean it a month before the weather's good enough to fish is up to something more than just rushing the season. He is engaged in invocation, visualization, and preparation for an act of hope and regeneration. Such profound implications can be drawn because fishing is largely an act of

31

faith, a gesture to luck and mystery that otherwise elude us during the more tedious and routine hours of our days. When we lower line, hook, and bait into the dark, unknown sea, we are engaged in an act of believing. The mere participation in such an act of uncertainty invigorates our spirits and allows us to surrender to the wisdom of the ages, nature, God, or whatever. Quite simply, fishing feels good to the soul.

What's more, though we always invoke fishing success with charms and habits, the illusion persists that if we have the best rods, reels, tackle, bait, and information, we can affect the outcome — which is true. After all, most fish aren't out to trick us, though we do transfer human traits to our prey as a matter of ancient record. Aboriginal cultures celebrate the transmigration of spirit into familiar sea creatures and so, unlike western Europeans, do not regard their prey as objects. The idea of inflicting pain and death for our own basic pleasure is repugnant to people who consider their spirits to be intertwined with fish.

You have to kill to eat meat, there's no doubt about that, but only from western Europe emerged the notion that you should do it for fun. Though wanton killing of fish is now frowned upon by the American sporting establishment, you have to wonder about its replacement, catch-and-release, which some extremists call torment-and-release.

Whether or not the morality of fishing for sport is defensible, its proliferation since World War II has brought with it rituals and totems that are primarily male in orientation and religious in tone. As though we need a reason to be in the wilderness, the splendor and solitude of a spring dawn on, say, a Montana creek has become not only literary in its resonance, but a matter of life support for a lot of people. Fishing trips are renowned for creating lifetime bonds of friendship and even matrimony.

At the end of the twentieth century, millions of people — men and women — really live to fish. And though the fish come up short because they get killed and eaten or thrash around at the end of a line, they have worked their way into our lives as modern totems. We take big ones home, iced down for the taxidermist, who doesn't stuff the fish at all but takes a mold off the carcass and discards the meat. We let a lot of them go, some die, some don't, some become yarns and tall tales, some get into books and onto T-shirts. We memorialize them in the form of swizzle sticks for our drinks, in paintings, as key rings, salt and pepper shakers, mailbox carvings, and tie tacks. An artist in California had his Land Rover painted to resemble a trout.

All the karmic wrong turns you can take as a sport fisherman, though, are easy to avoid for most commercial fishermen, particularly those who get out there and do it with hook-and-line gear similar to the sports. The best thing about fishing for a living is that most of the fish will end up on plates somewhere in the world, and somehow that equalizes the deal as long as you don't catch too much, which of course is the worst of all possible turns. You can't have less respect for an animal than to wipe out its entire species, something

that actually happens because of neglect and lack of knowledge about what goes on in the ocean.

A lot of commercial fishermen, like the trollers of the West Coast and Southeast Alaska who catch each salmon individually, clean it immediately, and pack it in ice to guarantee perfect quality, get a pretty good jolt of harmony out of their interaction with the fish. There are times when the sheer numbers of dead salmon on deck can put a rough edge on the proceedings. But generally, producing food in a respectful way keeps you straight with the spirit world and very much in tune with your prey.

With an intensity equal to that of the most compulsive and refined sport fisherman, trollers select their lures, lines, and baits, and submit constantly to the urge to try new colors, new techniques, and new places to remain competitive. They talk endlessly with other fishermen about what's working and what's not, about how to think like a salmon. The first rule of all fishing that settles on a troller like no other fisherman is: Find out what they want to eat and trick them with it. Almost all but the hard-core loners form groups with other trollers and talk on their radios in code to conceal their location and that of the best fishing.

A troller will tell you that each of five different salmon species has its own odor, that he catches more fish when he submits to his instinct as a predator and senses birds settling, current running, a change in atmospheric pressure that might send bait fish scurrying for the surface, or zooplankton to the bottom. He'll also tell you he's developed a perfectly timed swing of the gaff to kill the fish instantly while it's still in the water, and that even though fish turn into dollars at the dock, they hold endless fascination for him at sea.

Most trollers will admit they spend at least a few hours every season wondering just how they got so lucky to be getting paid for doing something they'd do for nothing. One of them, waxing eloquent in the Potlatch Bar overlooking Ketchikan harbor after a few jars of his favorite beverage, might even tell you the Pacific Ocean is a cathedral and fishing is a religion.

FISH HEAD, 1990.
Pastel, 22 x 17.

The Slime Line Survivor

Production work in the salmon packing trade is a deadly blend of despair and cheap thrills, sixteen-hour shifts in damp surroundings. The despair comes when you stand shoulder to shoulder with similarly distressed people and slit belly after belly of an endless supply of headless salmon, remove the guts, attempt humor by flipping the heart across the conveyor belt at some other poor soul, hose down the fish, then pick up another, and another, and another.

One cheap thrill comes in your pay envelope, an amount based on how many fish your crew managed to push through the plant that shift or

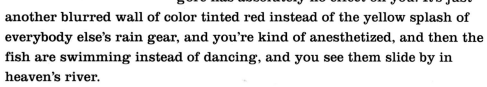

week. It's very direct stimulus and response, and just about everybody who gets into commercial fishing spends time on a slime line to make ends meet. The other, perhaps underrated cheap thrill starts at about hour eleven of the cruel sixteen when you can no longer deal with how bad your body hurts so you retreat into your mind and begin to see things that aren't there. Fish carcasses rise up like Disney characters and dance on their tails to the blaring rock 'n' roll from overhead speakers and the backbeat of the heading machine's thump, thump, thump. The gore has absolutely no effect on you. It's just another blurred wall of color tinted red instead of the yellow splash of everybody else's rain gear, and you're kind of anesthetized, and then the fish are swimming instead of dancing, and you see them slide by in heaven's river.

Just ask anybody who's done it.

"For he was astonished, and all that were with him, at the draught of fishes which they had taken." Luke 5:9

Left: *FISH HARD, DIE RICH*, 1987. Silk screen, 10 x 12.

Detail from *SOMETIMES LATE AT NIGHT THE SPIRITS OF ALL THE FISH I'VE EVER CAUGHT COME BACK TO HAUNT ME*, 1984. Pen, ink, and colored pencil, 8 x 12.

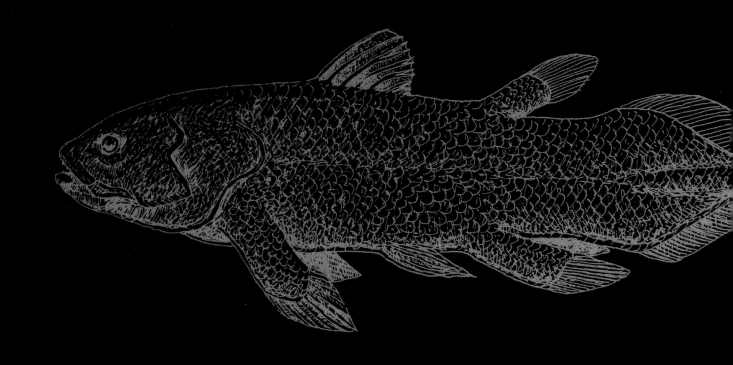

COELACANTH AT MIDNIGHT

F I S H   S T O R Y

TROLL '83

This is the monster halibut surfacing after a ten
hour fight - shortly before diving & snapping the line

FLATTENED BY A FLATFISH

Halibut are so
powerful many
fishermen on the
Pacific routinely
shoot fish over
100 pounds
before bringing
them into the
boat. Oddly, a
small halibut is
often calmed on
deck by rubbing
the white side of
its belly along
the lateral line,
a special sense
organ common to
most fish. The
same would
probably work
for bigger fish,
but you'd have a
hard time finding
somebody to do
the job.

Joe Cash came from the Dakota prairies to fish in Alaska and wore farmers' overalls on his boat, a funny old guy who got his nickname because he kept his cash in jars. He was also known for his fear of being eaten by crabs, and for sewing the buttons on his overalls with fishing line in the hope they wouldn't get at his body if he went overboard. Joe was finally killed by a halibut on his own boat deck, though, late in the season of 1973. What probably happened can be pieced together from the state trooper's report made when they fetched him.

Apparently, Joe hooked into a hog of a halibut off Kupreanof Island and landed the 150-pound brute with the proven technique of slipping a shark hook on a rope into its mouth, then shooting the fish in the head with a .22 pistol. Full of the elation that comes with a hundred-dollar fish, Joe must have reached down to free the hook when, suddenly, the great fish came alive.

The maddened slab of muscle then slammed its tail into the old man's legs and knocked him over. Joe's head struck the deck winch and he went out like a light, but the fish continued its primitive onslaught, broke both Joe's legs and severed an artery. Spent by the effort, the halibut died, and Joe Cash soon joined his fish on the other side. When a passing fisherman found his boat, *Flicka,* she was awash and aground on Eagle Point. Joe was dead, tied to the winch, his head above the water, the gaffed halibut at his feet. The crabs never got him.

Cuddling is a
fishing method
for those who
don't have the
stomach for
hooks. Cuddling
requires only
that you wade in
the water, sneak
up on your trout
or bass along
the bank, reach
under it and
grab it gently.
This is a proven
technique, but
you're not going
to get a lot of
volume with it.

Detail from
KISS A COHO, 1985.
Colored pencil, 4 x 5.

Following pages:
DOGS/CHUMS, 1984.
Colored pencil, 4½ x 9.

FISH LIPS

ALL THE RAGE

43

FAKE HUNTING AND THE BUSINESS OF FISH

WARM WATER, COLD DRINKS, AND CLEAN SHEETS

Fish are money-makers. For starters, you can write about them or draw pictures of them for a living, which generally attracts characters with questionable intentions. Much more profitably, you can catch them by the boatload, take them to shore, and sell them to somebody who will sell them again, and on down the line right to your favorite seafood bistro. That's been going on for centuries and is called commercial fishing, or bringing the fish to the consumer.

You can also bring the consumer to the fish, a far more recent and very lucrative phenomenon that includes a breathtaking web of charter boats, resorts, airlines; manufacturers of rods, reels, lures, line, boats, trailers, clothes, suntan lotion; and publishers of about twenty magazines on assorted fishing topics. It's hard to get a real handle on just how much the sport-fishing industry is worth in the high-flying America of the nineties, but you can figure about $20 billion a year.

Drawing the line is tough because nobody keeps records of fishing like they do automobile building. Clearly, you figure in the price of rods and reels, but how about the beer and motel and ice chest? Traditionally, the sports and commercials stretch the socioeconomic value of their fish-bucks so more congressmen will listen to them when they want to run each other off certain fishing grounds. While the number of people who want to eat or play with fish skyrockets, the number of fish stays about the same, meaning something's got to give.

If you think sport fishing is still just some tweedy guy at dawn on the Beaverkill lobbing a fly in an elegant wilderness ballet, check out one of the sportsmen's shows that make the rounds of the major cities in

In 1988, a sportsman from Alaska fishing off Hawaii was torn from his charter boat, still strapped in the fighting chair, and towed by a blue marlin to what he later estimated was eighty feet under water.

THRILL OF THE BILL,
1990.
Silk screen, 10 x 10.

winter. They're usually held in whatever domed stadium is handy and big enough to house hundreds, even thousands, of booths from which the sellers of the paraphernalia of sport fishing hawk their wares. The enterprises range from a ten-by-ten-foot niche in which a guy and his wife in matching shirts sell handmade lures arranged on a card table; to on-scene demonstrations by rod-makers, artists, and fly-tiers; to extravagant displays of great yachts, pantheons of outboards, and the entire inventories of flotation garment manufacturers.

The boom started in the sixties with the introduction of mass-produced fiber glass boats and jet airliners to the citizenry, who were finally given a real chance to take the leash off a vestigial hunting urge. By various estimates, the number of people who fish for the fun of fake hunting went from four million in 1955 to about twenty million in 1990, and the roster is growing every day.

Eventually the fish, exhausted from the onslaught, are going to say enough is enough. Meanwhile, the advent of the Saturday morning fishing program on TV and the videotape revolution have made fishermen out of folks who otherwise would have taken up wind surfing or off-road motorcycle riding. In the modern two-TV household, while the kids are zoned out on Saturday morning cartoons, Dad is watching *Bassin' for Bucks,* a half hour of a famous athlete and a professional bass fisherman casting into the lily pads from a $40,000 boat, talking in low voices like golf announcers. "Oh, yeah. That's it, you got him. Come on, Son. Here, let me get the net. Oh, yeah, that's a nice one. A guy doesn't see a better bass than that. Oh, yeah." Some programs include a segment with the bull-angler's wife showing viewers (or their wives) how to cook the catch, and all are backed by charter outfits or boat and tackle manufacturers, who tell you how easy it is to get your own bass boat, rod, and reel or take a trip to Belize to fish for tarpon on the flats.

Exotic destinations have become the clincher in modern fishing. A lot of people will tell you the casting, trolling, and catching are only incidental to a week in Isla Mujeres on the Yucatán, or Mazatlán, or Granada, or Panama, and the list goes on. At sporting shows and by mail-order through TV and magazine ads, you can buy self-seduction kits for big-game and distant-water fishing trips, also known as Fish Vids.

Typically, Fish Vids are of relatively low quality with background music like the soundtrack from one of those old-time travelogues on the Festival of the Children or something. They're often shot by amateurs who started out making home videos and became pros only when they found out how much money could be made taking pictures of marlin instead of fishing for them. You get a lot of unsteady camera work and the same patter as in *Bassin' for Bucks,* but, yahoo, you get a look at big fish that bend your mind in the direction of the airport.

If you do take the plunge and drop, say, $1,500 for three days at an exclusive fishing island in the Bahamas, or any one of hundreds of other remote locales starring marlin, sailfish, and tuna, you'll come to a full understanding of the addictive power of high-end sport fishing. Let's say you jet to Miami, where the resort's own plane picks you up for a hop across the near-shore crowds to Island **X**, a dry assertion of the vast Bahamian shoals that guard the continent, home to dark rum, warm winds, and very relaxed people, favored by pirates, gamblers, and fishermen. The Gulf Stream, a river within the sea, flows through and around the shoals, triggering upwellings of plankton, shrimp, and the other favorites of mackerel, ballyhoo and squid, which in turn are the prey of the great pelagics.

You arrive on the island in the evening and all is as advertised — friendly servants, cold drinks, clean sheets, and a fleet of those boats you can hardly believe exist, forty-eight feet long, with flared bows, air-conditioned salons, and smart captains. The first night in the subdued atmosphere around the pool or under the thatched eaves of the bar, you are

BASS ACKWARDS,
1988.
Silk screen, 12 x 10.

the new kid, silently nodding to the fish stories of those who have been there a day or two, the old hands, comrades of the hunt.

Then it's your turn. You rumble away from the dock before dawn with three other fishermen and the captain, a cook, and a mate, sipping grapefruit juice and nibbling on the smoked marlin from the boat's private stash. The run to where the fish were yesterday takes a couple of hours, so you fidget, talk, exchange life stories, and draw lots to see who gets the first turn in the fighting chair. The time comes, mercifully, when the mate streams the lines aft along the track of the rising sun, and the day is already hot. You were the lucky one and climb into the chair first, settling easily, naturally into the harness that will keep you in the boat when a big fish struggles with all its might to stay alive, your hook threatening otherwise. The Bahamian mate looks you over and nods, smiling a little, knowing that you feel like you never have before because he's seen many ordinary people become hunters for the first time.

Eight hours later, you will have caught a fish or not, but nobody ever asks for the money back.

CULT OF THE
RATFISH, 1985.
Pen, ink, and colored
pencil, 4 x 8.

*BEAR ATTACK AT
ART OPENING*, 1986.
Colored pencil, 7 x 8.

MACHO, MACHA

CATCHING THE BIG FISH

Size is relative. A two-pound trout is a big trout; a five-pound bass entitles you to a lot of bragging without benefit of falsehood; a fifty-pound salmon is mind altering. But don't think for a minute that your life won't change the instant you hook up with an eight-hundred-pound blue marlin or another of the true giants. A marlin the size of a mature zebra forever adjusts the way you relate to the idea of "fish."

In the early days of offshore angling for marlin, swordfish, tuna, and sharks, fishing clubs stationed physicians and nurses on their docks to greet returning fishermen, who frequently were injured fighting big fish. Men and women who partake of this dangerous ritual dip into parts of their psyches that not only can addict them to hunting big fish, but reinforce their validity as apex predators.

When you catch a big salmon, there is never any doubt that you and your lamiglass rod and bronze reel are up to the job. Your arms may get a little weary if the fight goes more than ten or fifteen minutes, but you never really feel at risk physically and even speak of "playing" the fish. With a small trout in a burbling brook it's even more of a waltz. When you are fast to a blue marlin, though, the gentle sense of artfulness departs at the moment of the strike. The fish doesn't just tug on the line, it transmits what feels like a vengeful kick to your arms and back, and the immediate fear engendered by pain sets in. Most consequentially, an encounter with one of the god-fish will last hours, not minutes, and you will never be the same.

Bears are no-limit salmon fishermen in the late summer when they come down from the forest to gorge themselves before slowing down for the winter. They stake out the same spots along streams every year and eat according to a family pecking order. Most of the time, though, they're vegetarians, getting by on roots, grass, and berries.

Professor Gilbert's Ghost

Under the threatening skies of a Seattle spring day, the Gilbert Ichthyological Society gathered to honor its namesake and worship fish. Their self-appointed task on this expedition was "to sort, identify, and catalog species at Archie McPhee's, a local trader in plastic fish who may be responsible for trafficking in rare and unusual specimens."

The society was founded in 1931 at the University of Washington, one of the great schools of fish, and reconstituted in 1989 to honor Charles Henry Gilbert, a son of the American West who was a major player in the rush to name the earth's creatures that dominated science in the nineteenth and early twentieth centuries. Gilbert eventually described and cataloged more than 30 percent of the fauna of the Northwest.

And so the society assembled in 1991, a dozen strong, in front of an emporium of kitsch and questionable taste, attired in masks and snorkels, lab coats, funny hats, and other fishy garb. One of them, Gilbert's biographer Gene Dunn, carried a portrait of the founder around the store, while others took specimens from shelves and bins, conducting themselves with scientific precision, their tongues planted firmly in their cheeks.

Later in the week, they gathered at the university's fish museum to identify their specimens and name the new species. The plastic collection, probably the only one of its kind in the world, would end up on the shelves among the dreamers, ratfish, sculpins, and 300,000 other marine miracles stored in jars of 70 percent ethanol.

By sad coincidence, the same week the society made their revolutionary move into the taxonomy of the plastic phyla, one species of salmon described by Professor Gilbert, the southernmost sockeye, was declared endangered, a victim of the dams on the Snake and Columbia rivers.

FISH WORSHIP, 1990.
Scratchboard, 7 x 8½

FISH STORY

I killed a snapper

First Fish Initiations

LUKE, I AM YOUR FATHER

Something indelible passes between elder and child in the drama of catching the first fish. Rites of passage imply an ordeal, but most of the time it is not so much in hooking and subduing a one-pound bass or the like as in the alien business of hauling a boat to the pond, fiddling with the intricate mysteries of rod, reel, casting, and waiting. Sensual programming ensues. If you happen to be on that bass pond in the South, the soft touch of spring wind carrying the aroma of pine needles banishes the dampness of early morning and the musty smell of the skiff. You will have risen at dawn because, like it or not, fish bite better in the morning. Part of the thrill, though, is getting up and creeping around the house, taking the lunches out of the refrigerator while mortals who will not participate in this momentous day can only dream on in their beds. And before your first fish, you may catch and touch a turtle, one of those repulsive amphibians with a layer of pond scum on its back. There are no first turtle stories.

Or in California, say, your father, mother, aunt, uncle, family friend, or any combination may drive you to the ocean, to a public fishing pier where you pay four dollars and take a post at the rail. Your immediate curiosity is about what the rest of the fishermen are using for bait and about what they have caught, which now occupies the bottoms of their plastic buckets under patches of wet burlap. This memory is punctuated by flashing gulls and terns, and the wildly graceful glides of pelicans, looking like prehistoric cartoon creatures as they sortie to inspect the leavings of bait and guano on the pier. Some birds work in shadows under the pier, making do with dropped sandwich scraps and the churning

I KILLED A SNAPPER,
1983.
Colored pencil, 8 x 6.

57

nourishment of the surf while, above, you are taught how to lower your hook to the water without tangling the line on the reel.

An emerging angler in the Pacific Northwest, off the Washingon coast for instance, may remember a moderate dose of fear wired into the excitement of lurching in a rented skiff on the morning chop, a little seasick from the motion and the noxious outboard fumes, but praying for a salmon to strike his carefully tuned herring. The rigging of the bait had been the subject of instruction, delivered as though luring a great salmon required not only skill but reverence. Many times, the young angler-to-be has been the beneficiary of salmon from the expeditions of neighbors and relatives in Seattle or Juneau or Astoria, who proudly displayed their catch on the lawn or in the sink. But now, maybe . . .

And the moment of truth comes, always, unannounced and at the time you least expect it, the bite so firm and clear you know you have a real fish and that it almost pulled the rod from your hands. On the pond, the stern tug of a bass through a light rod is every bit the challenge of a tuna's slashing attack to the pier initiate or the urgent singing of the reel when a salmon takes the bait and runs. You must fight the instinctive urge to yank hard on the rod, bringing instead an unnatural delicacy to the setting of the hook.

Whatever the prey, the young angler endures the coaching and excitement of his elder, who is ecstatic but intensely focused on the primitive chore at hand. Likely, the child has never seen such a version of his mother or father, so fully revealed, and might recall the moment as one in which the parent's love and approval, if ever tentative, was certain.

The end of the ceremony has three variations: either you eat the fish after you catch it, let it go, or, sadly, it expires for no good purpose. Some powerful circuit has been completed when the trout that rose to the flash of your spinner on the chrome surface of a Montana brook minutes later reposes, crackling in bacon fat, over a campfire on a sandbar. "You are like me," the elder has said, "a bringer of food."

A lot of rivers are "Catch and Release" only, which means anglers can hook the fish, but not keep and eat them. On one such popular beat on an Alaska river, the trout, they say, have been caught and released so many times they don't have lips any more.

CUTTHROAT BUSINESSMEN, 1988. Pen, ink, and watercolor, 8 x 6.

Following pages: ONE SHOT JACK, 1988. Mixed media, 9½ x 21.

E SHOT JACK

ONE TRIP UPSTREAM

RAY TROLL 1988

SALMON CELEBRITY

One summer late in the eighties, a king salmon on the Kenai River in Alaska helped affirm, once again, Andy Warhol's pronouncement: Everybody gets to be famous for fifteen minutes. In this case, it was more like two days, but the story involved a very ordinary tourist from the Midwest, a couple of guides, a giant fish, and riverbanks of shoulder-to-shoulder anglers, at least one of whom showed up with his video camera.

From June to August, traveling the two-lane blacktop from Anchorage to Homer is known as Winnebago roulette because the traffic is so thick and dangerous. Edging out to pass at the wrong split-second can turn you into a road kill. (In the winter, the moose take over for the RVs.) The highway from Anchorage nicks the river in a couple of spots, producing combat fishing on some stretches — grotesque scenes of flailing rods, tangled lines, beer coolers, jousts with landing nets, unruly children, and the unpleasant company of morning drinkers.

To escape the battle on the banks, some anglers hire guides and drift boats to cruise the center line of the river and add a floating twist to the parody of fishing. It was in one of these boats that the drama was

SOCKEYE KILLER,
1990.
Silk screen, 10 x 10.

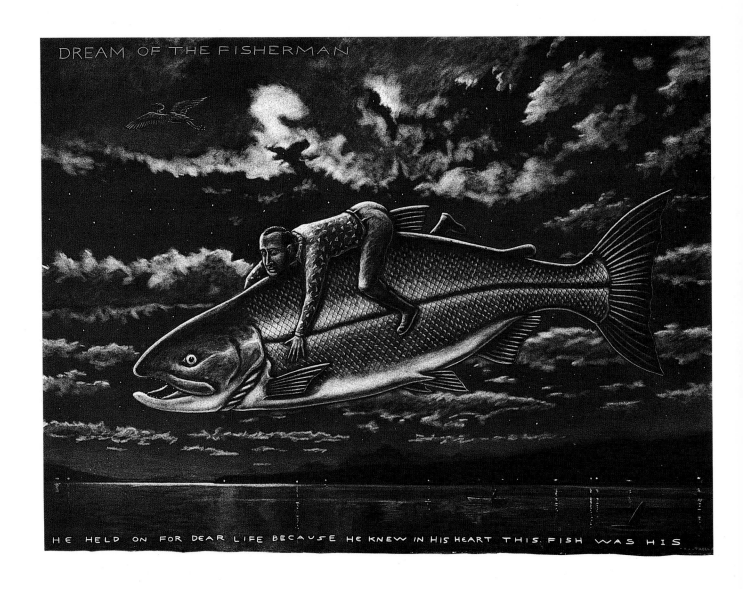

DREAM OF THE FISHERMAN

HE HELD ON FOR DEAR LIFE BECAUSE HE KNEW IN HIS HEART THIS FISH WAS HIS

DREAM OF THE
FISHERMAN, 1987.
Charcoal, 22 x 30.

played, beginning when the sixty-ish fellow hooked up with a salmon that obviously would require no lying. The fish towed the boat, snagging lines from the banks and other boats, but generally creating the goodwill a big fish can engender among observing anglers, so everybody was rooting for the guy. Somebody started shooting a videotape, and perhaps anxious for his own moment of fame, rushed it into Anchorage that afternoon for the evening news. Later that night, the TV station sent a crew to the river, where, twelve hours into the fight, the spectacle of man and salmon had so captivated everybody that most quit fishing in the late arctic light that gives you twenty-hour days. On the banks, they just watched.

The next day, the Anchorage station offered its tape on the satellite feed to stations around the country, and the salmon celebrity emerged with all the hoopla of the rescue of a little girl from a Texas well a few months before. The nation was treated to images of bent rod, nervous guide, and exhausted angler against the background of the annual orgy on the Kenai. Every infotainment newscast for a day and a half used the salmon and its would-be subduer as its good-news feature. On the morning of the second day, we actually got a look at the beast as the angler eased the great fish to the side of the boat and the guide tried and failed to net it. The salmon was simply too big for the net and, with sullen dismissal implied in the splash of its massive tail, churned up a frothy wake and a hump in the water surface as it ran for its life.

The official world record for salmon on sport gear is under 100 pounds, and this fish was surely bigger than that, so the fisherman and his guides were careful to observe the rules of the record-keeping International Game Fish Association. Only the angler could touch the rod or no record. The TV showed the man trying to sleep, eat, and finally just about hallucinating in the thirty-six hours he was fast to the fish.

In the dim light of late evening on the second day, the scene with the net at the boat was repeated, only this time the line broke and the salmon went free. The angler and his guides were too tired to show much emotion, looking curiously relieved and pathetically mortal in the glare of the television lights. The angler, when asked for his comment on losing the fish of fish, said: "I guess I wasn't supposed to catch it." The guide had tears in his eyes.

The Buzz Bomb, a legendary fish catcher in the Pacific Northwest, is one of the most deadly lures ever invented because it appeals to the lateral lines of its victims, special fish-only sensory organs that alert the salmon, trout, or steelhead to motion nearby. The lateral line is far more important to fish than their senses of sight, smell, or touch. We humans lost our lateral lines when our ancestors left the ocean . . . but maybe not, thus explaining good vibes and bad vibes.

DOG DAY AFTERNOON, 1987. Colored pencil, 30 x 22.

DOG DAY AFTERNOON

No Free Lunch

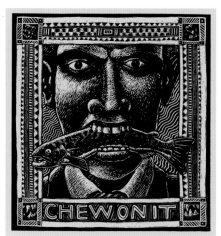

CHEW ON IT, 1990.
Scratchboard, 5 x 5.

Opposite page:
BIG BITE, 1988.
Oil pastel and crayon,
32 x 40.

Earthlings increased their annual catch of seafood from 20 million tons to 100 million tons between 1950 and 1990. It's hard to imagine that much fish, so for comparison, a VW camper weighs about a ton, or 2,000 pounds. Figure we catch and eat something like the equivalent of 100 million campers if you need something you can visualize. The really big news, though, is that everybody who knows-it-all about the ocean says we'll never take more than 100 million tons — never mind earlier reports that the bounty of the sea was unlimited and capable of dealing with Tom Malthus's pessimistic conclusions about people out-reproducing their food supply.

At the same time we were getting positively ravenous for food from the ocean, our own numbers increased from two and a half billion souls to five and a half billion. By 2030, the scorecard will read something like

I HAVEN'T HAD A BITE ALL DAY

eleven billion, barring a weeding out of breeding males or some such catastrophe. So Malthus was right after all, and the ocean won't bail us out: population increases exponentially, food supply increases mathematically.

Between 1970 and 1990, Americans became seafood eaters of note, raising their annual consumption from about eight pounds per mouth-to-feed to fifteen pounds. By comparison, real fish eaters like the Japanese eat something like a hundred and fifty pounds each every year. What happened in the U.S.A. was that people figured out the fish was delicious for reasons that go beyond building your dogma bank account at the

Vatican by eating no meat on Friday, which really is what all fish dealers based their marketing strategy on as late as 1970. We also served up some technological voltage in the form of quick freezing, air freight, and marketing that gave seafood a good name.

In the mid-seventies, however, it seemed like every chef and supermarket buyer was fish crazy and fear-of-bones-in-the-throat gave way to blackened redfish, fresh exotics like monkfish, orange roughy airlifted from Australia, and live tanks so you could pick out your dinner while it was still on the hoof, or fin. Nobody seemed to notice that you couldn't possibly stand to do the same thing to a lamb or baby cow, pick it out and eat it that night; but the general sense about fish was and is that they don't look back at you and they never quit coming. A lot of people relate to fish like they're vegetables with eyes.

The worst thing to happen since seafood became a designer food in America is that heavily promoted species like redfish and rockfish and snapper are in danger of joining the ranks of the fossils. Those fish and a lot of their tasty cousins are often very long lived and not at all prolific. Replacing a 150-year-old rockfish takes some doing, not to mention a fair dose of irreverence. Long lives and modest reproductive box scores mean you can nail a single generation and the survivors just can't muster enough oomph as a group to keep the species viable. When the delicacies of the sea are gone, blackened tofu and bean cake sushi aren't going to thrill the gourmands.

A lot of people figure we can use the sea and inland water as a big farm or ranch to raise what we need to eat. It's happening already, but there's a limit to how much nourishment nature can produce or absorb and stay balanced; we'll probably run into some limits like we have with wild seafood. Sea farms now grow oysters, clams, mussels, salmon, abalone, shrimp, trout, and other top-dollar seafood. From ponds on land, we're getting trout, catfish, shrimp, and tilapia (a.k.a. African lake fish).

With a little luck, some new way of making food will hold Malthus and the population spoilsports at bay. Meanwhile, Grandfather Rockfish is getting taken to lunch, maybe for the last time. The next time he arrives, steaming on your plate, remember to say thanks and find out who caught him and where he used to live.

Detail from
FISH WARS, 1985.
Mixed media, 30 x 38.

Something like 200 trillion pounds of seafood ring the cash register in global trade every year. Fish buyers, sellers, and brokers tend to be a ruthless clan, constantly alert to betrayal since their goods are highly perishable and payment depends on condition on delivery. There's no more nervous seller than one with, say, a quarter of a million pounds of dover sole on trucks between Seattle and Los Angeles during a heat wave, with only half their payment up front.

MIGS AND TURBOT,
1985.
Colored pencil, 12 x 15.

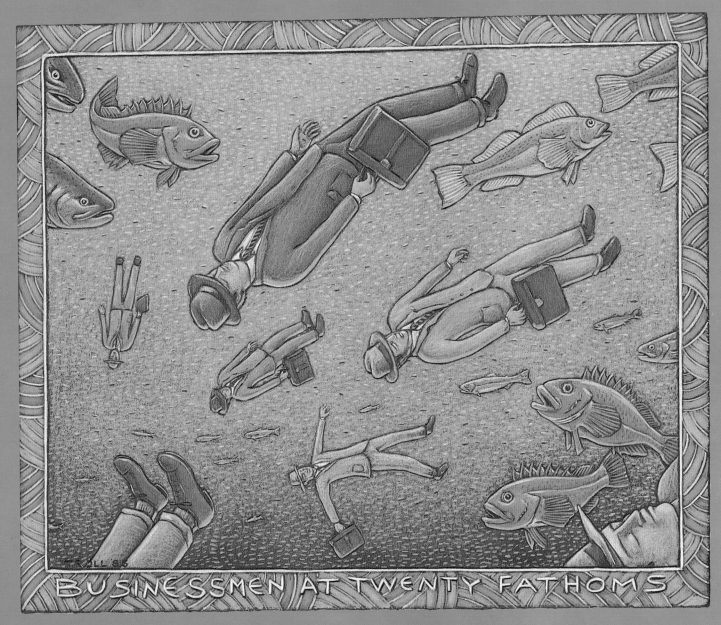

BUSINESSMEN AT
TWENTY FATHOMS,
1986.
Colored pencil, 8½ x 10.

HOW FISH DO IT

In late summer, the hottest ticket for tourists stopping in Juneau, Alaska, gets them aboard a bus for a half-hour ride north to Mendenhall Glacier, a cascade of ancient ice ending its frozen epoch in a drive-up delta of creeks and streams. Any other time of year, the buses head straight for the parking lot at the glacier visitor center, from which folks get a look at crystal blue ice and hear how much noise something the size of Bakersfield makes sliding in slow motion over rocks and gravel.

BREATHING, EATING, AND ROMANCE

Along about mid-August, though, this is humpy country. The capillaries made by the melting ice are alive with spawning salmon, in from the Pacific to hurl themselves upstream in main watercourses and in tributaries sometimes only inches deep.

And in the upper reaches of the creeks, the spawned-out salmon begin to come apart. Flesh peels off their flanks, fins are left behind; pieces of jaw, teeth, and cartilage litter the shallows; and their bodies are gone to bleached bones almost before they are dead. Eagles, ravens, and bears rejoice at the easy pickings.

So the cruise ship buses pull off along the road to give the customers a close-up look at real life, fish style. "The smell is revolting," is the most common observation, but a close second is: "It's so sad, they only get one shot at it." And it would be, if these orange, red, and purple hallucinations of fish were, instead, a gowned and tuxedoed couple making the long walk to the preacher. The pathos is intensified because everybody knows salmon return to the streams of their birth to spawn. But no, it isn't sad if you're a salmon, one of few fish that even show the difference between boys and girls without being cut open and given a gonad exam. Male and female salmon turn different colors when they spawn, and some species change shapes.

SPAWN TIL YOU DIE,
1987.
Pen, ink, and colored
pencil, 11 x 7½.

The male pink, or humpy, turns into a nightmare of itself, its backbone arching (hence the nickname), its jaw shaping into a formidable weapon with protruding teeth for the final battles against competing males. The female, her physiology much more intact than the male's, scoops out a little gravel nest called a redd with her rapidly disappearing tail. Here she deposits thousands of eggs for the suitor cruising in full bloom alongside, who is ready to squeeze his milt into the water at the moment most perfect for fertilization. There is no blushing on the creek bottom, no coy demurring, and once you get past the horror of dissolving fish, spawning looks like the clean dance of life it is.

Nature is full of grim truths and somehow sex without touching is one of the worst. Fish romance is often just a matter of statistical luck: males and females do their own thing in the same general area with good odds that if enough of them show up, some eggs will get lucky. Certain fish, like black bass, don't even need an opposite sex to reproduce; each one is the whole show itself. Others begin life as males and end up as females, participating in reproductive rites as both. Almost all fish lay eggs — the big word is oviparous — but some, like the surf perch, bear young alive like us, making them viviparous. And some are ovoviviparous, like sharks and rays, which means they produce eggs that are hatched within the mother and remain there until live, fully-formed fish are born.

Tilapia lay eggs in the mouths of their mates, where they hatch and, if the young fish don't leave their parent's mouth when they're supposed to, they're dinner. Now that's an unhappy childhood. Other fish build nests and then decoy the opposite sex into them with gaudy displays by actually changing skin color. Most fish skin is live cells all the way to the surface, unlike our own, and they have slime layers to keep them waterproof and free of cell-penetrating disease. (That's why you wet your hands before you touch a fish, unless you intend to kill and eat it.)

The color cells used in reproductive attraction, called chromatophores, are most useful to a fish for passive defense, since it is a meal as much as a predator and becoming invisible to something that wants to eat you is a good piece of work. A plaice, for instance, can change not only the colors of its body but also the patterns of its markings. Put a plaice on a checkered tablecloth and you'll get a checkered plaice. Some

BIG FISH, BIG CITY, BIG DEAL, 1990. Pen, ink, and colored pencil, 22 x 17.

74

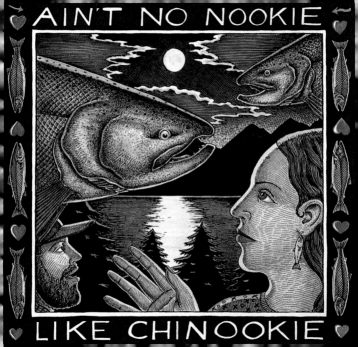

fish have photophores that actually produce light, like the dwellers of the abyss, which use their lanterns to attract meals in the dark water. Others use their chromatophores to signal attack or fear, like the marlins and swordfish, which flash blue, purple, and fierce red when threatened.

Reproduction is job one, but job two is survival: eating and breathing. Eating is the easiest to understand since most fish are pretty much like us with a stomach, intestine, and the waste discharge organs — liver, kidneys, and bladder. Their digestive tracts are usually very acidic, beginning with the mouth, and they can easily dissolve a fishhook. Fish have developed the physiology to accommodate those food sources most abundant around them, so you have flesh eaters with teeth, shell eaters with beaks, plant eaters with strainers, and fish that absorb nutrients with suckers and an external stomach. None of that is too hard to grasp.

Breathing under water is a tantalizing fantasy, and it is the ability of fish to draw oxygen from water that is probably most responsible for our intense fascination with them. All of us have imagined a magic transformation to allow us to breathe water, but even scuba divers don't get close. The critical factor is the most obvious: air is a gas, water is a liquid.

Enter, gills. The exchange of oxygen for carbon dioxide is called respiration. We do it by bringing air into our chests where it comes in contact with porous lung membranes, through which the oxygen moves into our blood, and carbon dioxide back out. Gills are kind of like external lungs over which water passes, offering oxygen for extraction in far smaller quantities than air breathing. A fish's blood carries the oxygen from the gills to the rest of the body and returns carbon dioxide. Some fish are one up on us when it comes to breathing, too, since they can also extract oxygen from air.

A pretty spectacular bit of anatomy called a gas bladder accounts for a fish's air breathing trick, a bag under its kidney that produces noise, adjusts buoyancy, and in tarpon, gars, and some other fish, lets the fish breathe like you and me. Not all fish have gas bladders, but those that do have to surface occasionally to gulp air, and since the bladder is surrounded by a web of blood vessels, oxygen is absorbed. That's not surprising. After all, we began our evolutionary rhumba in the sea and not the other way around.

WEIRD AND SCARY FISH

SHARKS, RAYS, AND BIG, BIG HEADS

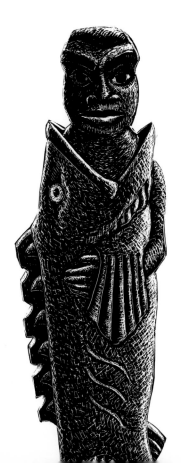

Imagine the shock when Jacques Picard and Donald Walsh eased their bathyscape *Trieste* to the bottom at 35,800 feet in the Mariana Trench and saw, in the searchlight of their craft, a flatfish of some kind loaf lazily away. The aquanauts were deeper into the abyss than humans had ever been, and nobody expected them to find life in the primordial ooze of that dark, lonely, cold region of the sea. Victorian biologists had even asserted that absolutely no life could exist below 1,800 feet. They were way, way off, but probably in their wildest phantasms could not have come close to describing what does live in the abyss.

The oceans are as deep in parts as Mount Everest is high, about seven miles, and tribes of fish and other twists of life evolved down there just like everyplace else, perfectly suited for survival and reproduction. Even the shallow parts of the abyss are like the world's worst resort for meeting a boyfriend if you're, say, a female smooth dreamer *(Chaenophryne parviconus)*, a roundish monster about three inches long with a mouth half the size of your body and a fishing-rodlike ornament growing out of your head, with a lantern on the end, that's used to lure food — which is about as scarce as dance partners. To solve the mate problem without makeup, smooth dreamers and their cousins take a real hard line on divorce. The males are about a fifth the size of the females and become permanently attached to their brides, absorbing nutrients right through their blood. This setup is not at all uncommon down there and has a lot to do with the complete absence of light, like the big heads, which have to do with the odds that you'll cover enough water with a snap to catch something in the dark.

79

To get anywhere at all in the dating department, as well as the eating department, deep-water creatures have evolved organs of light, triggered — even at will — by the oxygen in their blood. There's plenty of oxygen in the deeps because polar circulation drives cold, oxygenated water down, and the pressure of up to four tons per square inch is no problem because the force is the same inside and out. Fish born down there have parchment-thin skin and wispy bones, but those boys in the bathyscape, with air pockets in every bit of their bodies, would be crushed like smacked gnats.

Abyssal creatures use light to attract mates and prey and to defend themselves by signaling size to a predator. It's reasonable to assume that a modestly lit but extremely ugly *Lasiognathus saccostoma,* no matter how hungry, won't mess with a six-foot *Chrisotomias photopterus* flashing like the Goodyear blimp at minus ten thousand feet. Even with the weird results delivered by evolution, the shapes and organs of the abyssal fish follow the basic rules: reproduce and eat, no matter how mean or ugly you have to be.

Some fish are still puzzles that way, like an especially mean one closer to home that is reputed to have killed Ulysses. The great stingrays (*Trygon*) of the tropics, some with wingspreads of ten feet or more, have poisonous barbs at the end of long, whiplike tails that don't seem to do them much good against anything but humans, who were definitely not part of the stingray's early evolutionary picture.

The rays are most closely related to sharks in the family of fish that are hung together with cartilage instead of bones, the *chondrichthyoids.* Sharks, of course, are serious trouble at times because they are big and they bite, a rough combination if you happen to be a seaborne human like that one off Point Dume in California in the late eighties who was yanked out of his kayak and off into eternity by a Great White, just like the one in *Jaws.* Though the attack was not likely amorous in intent, sharks are known as claspers as far as reproduction goes, and they get to touch each other when they make babies. Fish such as the glorious ratfish, related to sharks because their skeletons are cartilage, too, are also claspers.

The fact remains, though, that most fish, no matter where they live, are absolutely harmless to humans.

SHOCKING PINKS,
1985.
Pastel, 22 x 30.

DO FISH DREAM?

Who knows? They don't have eyelids, so you have to wonder if they even sleep, especially judging from the way they're always on the prowl in an aquarium. But fish don't have to spend as much energy as land animals to regulate body temperature, produce water, find food, reproduce, and fight gravity, so they don't need much rest. They do go into a kind of trance of inactivity resembling sleep once in a while, but with their eyes open.

Maybe they have some way of drawing the shades inside their little brains if their eyes are on duty all the time. Fish eyes are pretty amazing. First of all, they are spherical so a fish can see all around without swiveling the neck it doesn't have. For another thing, most fish eyes see different things at the same time, which would be real confusing to humans, whose eyes integrate imagery into a single picture. Fish use the same eye technology as humans, with rods and cones in varying proportions, depending on the intensity of the light where the owner lives. Deep-water, dim-light fish have almost no cones, only rods.

Maybe fish just don't stop seeing when they sleep. Some settle into lazy stupors for hours or weeks, and in that condition they can be further hypnotized and actually lifted out of the water. If you come upon a trout hovering in a shallow brook in the warmth of midday, for instance, reach down and gently tickle its back, carefully, until you sense it relaxing even more. You'll be sending it to never-never land, maybe into a dream or some kind of trout hallucination of being a bird.

ONE FISH, TWO FISH,
DEAD FISH,
BLUE FISH, 1985.
Pastel and colored
pencil, 34 x 18.

Following pages:
SNAPPERS IN LOVE,
1984.
Colored pencil, 4 x 7½.

83

SNAPPE

RS IN LOVE

MIDNIGHT JUMPERS,
1984.
Colored pencil, 6½ x 8.

ICHTHYOSOPHY

STRUNG OUT ON FISH

Admitting you're obsessed with fish isn't easy, especially since there aren't any support groups or meetings you can go to, or therapists who specialize in fish addiction. How does a guy like Ray Troll tell his kids he's spent eight hours a day for ten years drawing pictures of fish, filling up notebooks and scratch pads with endless renditions of ratfish, long ago abandoning the pretense that metaphor has anything to do with it? Some of us are just different, I guess, but it seems like a lot more people are tumbling to fish life of one kind or another, losing control with our finny neighbors.

THE ARCHFISHOP

It used to be that only the sports like fly-fishermen took a bad rap for the single-mindedness that fish worship can bring, but now the club has widened to include artists, chefs, biologists, jewelers, writers, moviemakers, interior decorators, comedians, and hucksters of every stripe. I think the big turn was that somebody figured out you didn't have to kill or even eat fish to get involved. Every big city has a great aquarium now, real extravaganzas with tony politicians on the boards of directors and gift shops full of fish-love paraphernalia that are real gold mines. You have to wait in line for hours just to get into some of them, like the one in Monterey, where they brought a whole kelp forest full of fish inside. Any doubt that fish are the in-critters is banished when you realize there are even dozens of magazines on just fish — how to catch them, how to cook them, how to keep them in tanks in your living room, how to sell them, how to understand them. Where will it end?

The hardworking belted kingfisher, common to most of North America, is nature's fish planter as well as a voracious consumer. If you've ever wondered how fish get into landlocked lakes and ponds, imagine a kingfisher snatching a likely candidate from ocean waters, heading inland, and dropping the fish at just the right time. It's a statistical long shot, but over centuries ponds and lakes grow richer.

ASSAULT FROM THE AIR, 1987.
Mixed media, 26 x 40.

Habitat Is Where It's At

GROWING UP FISH

When you think about how hard it is to get to be a steelhead in the Columbia River, it's a wonder any of them make it. First, you're a fertilized egg in a pocket of gravel on the bottom of a tributary stream somewhere, and if you're lucky the timber is still standing on the banks and nearby hills. If it's gone to make gum wrappers, cardboard boxes, or subdivisions, the stream will fill up with silt from erosion and that's all she wrote for you and the rest of the salmon and steelhead eggs. And when the parent fish get back the next year, they're not going to find any place to cuddle, either.

The next big test in your steelhead childhood comes after your egg develops an eye and you turn into an actual little fish with fins and everything. Birds and other fish already will have eaten a bunch of your cousins, and that's going to keep on, like it or not. If you last until you're about two or three inches long, though, you have to start thinking about the turbines in the dams downstream. You're an anadromous fish, and that means you head out to the Big O to spend most of your life because that's where the living is easy — salt water that doesn't freeze, lots of food, no bears, eagles, and like that. The trouble is that between you and the ocean are about ten dams, each rigged with turbines that churn like giant Cuisinarts making salmon and steelhead puree.

Always, you have to worry about not getting eaten, and about where your next meal grew up itself. The closer you get to the coast, the more birds, seals, sea lions, and bigger fish you have to deal with, and the more trouble you can get into eating a herring or needlefish that's been hanging around a pulp mill or sewer outfall someplace sucking up PCBs or petroleum sludge. Finally, if you survive all that, you cruise for a couple

In the Territory of Alaska, eagles and Dolly Varden were considered varmints, subject to bounties because they ate salmon eggs and fry. To get paid, you just had to bring proof of your kill down to the Fish and Game, and a lot of kids earned their first dollars on talons and tails.

PRESERVE THE BALANCE, 1989. Pen, ink, and acrylic, 9½ x 8.

91

or three years out in the ocean, grow up, then head back through the same mess to try to score in the stream of your birth — if it's still there.

Steelhead share stream and nearshore habitat in common with about 90 percent of the fish we depend on for food and sport. In the relative shallows of the coastal zone, light penetrates to invigorate the water column from top to bottom, producing a wonderful chow line of plant and animal plankton, and every kind of fish from there up. It's a great place for a fish to raise a kid, and that's why beaches, bays, and estuaries are so critical to keeping the ocean food web intact.

The problem is that waterfront occupation by the booming human population destroys the rearing areas for several stages in the food web. When you trash the sardines in southern California by either catching all of them or building Los Angeles, you also kill off the marlin, swordfish, tuna, and on and on and on. It's not hard to figure out what to do: don't dump poison in the ocean and don't destroy estuaries by filling them in to build shopping malls.

For a long time we thought the ocean was a great garbage disposal, and for things that disintegrate it still is. Plastic, however, and other engineered substances last hundreds, even thousands of years and you only have to visit one beach near a city to know what that means. About 85 percent of the pollution of the ocean comes from what we do on land, and we also now know that almost all of that never leaves the coast. Getting to be a steelhead is harder and harder every year.

FISH FACTS, 1989.
Pen, ink, and
watercolor, 6 x 8.

A spawning
salmon will swim
as far as 3,000
miles up a river
like the Yukon or
the Columbia,
and then turn
into a monster to
have sex.

94

HUMPIES FROM HELL,
1984.
Colored pencil, 7½ x 9.

Deep, Deep Thoughts

The possibility that we humans are fouling up the old globe beyond our ability to repair it seems to be on everybody's mind these days, probably because a decrepit version of creation theory has expired, wheezing and gasping in the corner of the shack where we store our collective wisdom. The idea that something, somewhere, set up earth just to provide for human comfort and sustenance won't wash any more. Most of us no longer see ourselves at the top of the natural heap, but pretty much as equal performers in a cosmic balancing act with the fish, birds, trees, and other life-forms.

Nobody likes the pathetic notion that humans are the destroyer species, so a lot of enlightened thought is going into figuring out better ways to behave. One of our most recent flashes of insight has to do with trying to determine just when the soup of life is souring, and we've come up with the notion of "indicator species." The theory is akin to the practice of toting canaries into mine shafts to give miners an edge if the air became tainted with poison gas from an unseen source. When the birds quit singing, or worse, keeled over in their cages, the miners headed for the surface.

We don't have an exit from our mine shaft if things go real bad, no place to run to, but at least we're no longer kidding ourselves. One thing is for sure: water makes earth the paradise it is. Fish are our canaries, and a lot of them are missing a few notes or hacking between verses. So do a good turn for a Pacific spiny lumpsucker today.

NAVIGATION WITHOUT NUMBERS, 1988. Colored pencil and watercolor, 10 x 8.

Most fish have sniffer systems a thousand times keener than those of dogs. A bass, for instance, can smell one part per trillion, or, in martini equivalents, roughly one drop of vermouth in five hundred thousand barrels of gin.

KELP FOREST II, 1988. Colored pencil and crayon, 30 x 22.

"Buddha is like
the great river.
The fish of other
teachings swim about
in its depths."
The Teaching
of Buddha

BETWEEN THE DEVIL
AND THE DEEP BLUE
SEA, 1986.
Colored pencil, 7½ x 9.

ACKNOWLEDGMENTS I'd like to thank the zany, creative crew who put this book together and made it such an enjoyable experience: Marlene Blessing, Brad Matsen, Kate Thompson, and Carl Smool. Sincere thanks as well to the Troll family, and especially my wife, Michelle, for supporting my artistic endeavors. I feel a real sense of indebtedness to the following cast of characters, in no particular order: Gaylen Hansen, Linda Okazaki, Carl Chew, Jim and Jo Hockenhull, Israel Shotridge, the Tongass Tribe, the Native peoples of the Northwest and Alaska for their awe-inspiring art, Candia Coombs and my eco-pals, Mr. A's Lunch Club, Lillian Ference, Bill Spear, Tom Sadowski, Mr. Whitekeys, Mark Winward and the entire gang at Quality Classics Sportswear, Mystic Lane Shirt Company, Bill Ellis, Kent Lovelace, those wild Abajian brothers, the Stonington Gallery folks, George Estrella, the surrealist fishmongers at Silver Lining Seafoods, my Ketchikan/Seattle/Kansas circle of friends, Corinna and Patrick, and all my finny brethren.

R. T.

While I was writing this book, a lot of people provided me with hospitality, support, true facts, and light. Any errors are mine, not theirs. Thanks to: Marlene Blessing, Ray Troll, Kate Thompson, Carl Smool; the crew at National Fisherman; Frank D'Amor, the staff, and volunteers at the Port Townsend Marine Science Center; Lex Snyder, Ted Pietsch, and the rest of the Gilbert Ichthyological Society; Thomas von Bahr; Bill Spear; Krys Holmes and Laara Estelle.

B. C. M.

For further information about Ray Troll's T-shirts and more,
contact Quality Classics, 1-800-735-7185.

Many other fascinating books
are available from Alaska Northwest Books™.
Ask at your favorite bookstore or write us for a free catalog.

Alaska Northwest Books™
A division of GTE Discovery Publications, Inc.
P.O. Box 3007
Bothell, Washington 98041-3007
Call toll free 1-800-343-4567